ALPHABITE SOUP FOR BUSINESS

ROSS S MITCHELL

Copyright © 2025 by Ross S Mitchell, Nesso - Inspiring Visionary Leaders All rights reserved. No part of this book may be reproduced in any manner whatsoever without written permission except in the case of brief quotations embodied in critical articles and reviews.
First Printing, 2025

ALPHABITE SOUP FOR BUSINESS

EAT AS MUCH OR AS LITTLE AS YOU NEED

"Whatever your reason for being in business my hope for you is that the sun shines brightly on your face and that you have fair wind at your back"
- Ross Mitchell

As a business coach, Ross Mitchell has the uncanny knack, of making complex business concepts simple.

Ross has often been heard to say that business is not rocket science and that anyone, could be a business coach, that it was only common sense. And most of us know that common sense, is not so common.

Ross has worked with hundreds of business owners and managers, to help unlock the secrets, to their next phase of growth.

The idea of Alphabite Soup for Business, is to allow the reader to understand, develop and apply a common sense approach to business, by taking little bites, to find immediate solutions or inspiration, or for those people, who are looking to accelerate their career, or business venture, by taking on as much as they can, as quickly as possible and as slowly as necessary.

Table of Contents

Dedicated to	7
Introduction	9
Testimonials	13
4 is for	15
A is for	17
B is for	21
C is for	27
D is for	37
E is for	43
F is for	45
G is for	49
H is for	51
I is for	55
J is for	59
K is for	61
L is for	63
M is for	65
N is for	67
O is for	69
P is for	71
Q is for	73
R is for	75
S is for	79
T is for	85
U is for	91
V is for	93
W is for	95
X is for	97
Y is for	99
Z is for	101
Where to Next? The Final Word	105
About The Author	109
Acknowledgements	111
Three Letter Acronyms-	113

Dedicated to

To my amazing partner in life, Shauna, you are my rock.

Ashlee and Sam, thank for your love and patience.

To my Dad Jack, who has always been there with an honest ear, always telling me as it is. Thank you, for being who you are.

I am blessed to have many great friends, who have seen me through thick and thin, you know who you are!

To each of you, I am proud to be part of your lives and grateful for your support.

Introduction

So here you are…… you have an idea, you want to start a business and be the next Bill Gates, Elon Musk or Colonel Sanders, live a great life, live rich, make heaps of cash and fashionably, leave a legacy.

"To you I dips me lid!"

It was said, that people who fail to learn from mistakes of the past, are destined to repeat them, in the future.

But when you are starting your life and business journey, and presumably, haven't made that many mistakes, how can you expect to have a bruise free run at business. To some extent, you can't, nor should you.

With that said, it makes some sense, to pay attention to what some people, who have gone before you, have encountered, learnt from, capitalised on and similarly not learnt from and then paid the price.

In today's society, Grey hair and middle age, are not always appreciated, although when they are present, they have nearly always come with, a great many scars and produced some wisdom. It is this wisdom that I wish to impart upon you, to help you, avoid some of the scars that you may be about to, or have already achieved, as you pound your way, through the journey, as a business owner / operator/ entrepreneur.

The reasons for wanting to start a business, are likely to vary from person to person, from age to age and at various points in your maturation.

Your reasons are yours. At least I hope that they are.

You may be straight out of school and have seen your parents work tirelessly, at a job they are only moderately satisfied with, hate or love, are successful at, but are never home and you don't want to repeat, what they have done.

You might already have been working for people, for several years and feel that nobody is listening, the boss is a fool, making too much money that they don't spread around, to you and your colleagues, they do a rubbish job, they aren't brave enough, to take on the great ideas, you have and on it goes.

Or you might just have something, that you know, in your heart of hearts, you want to do, sell or make, that you believe people want or need.

Whatever your reasons, for wanting to start, congratulations and take a bow. Because whoever, wherever, whatever you are, there are another 10 people, who have thought like you and for their own reasons, have not had the courage to do what you are about to do.

To provide some context.

My career started as an 11-year-old, delivering the local newspaper The Chadstone Progress, once a week for the princely sum of $2.27 per week. Come rain, hail or shine (and in Melbourne, Australia that could be on the same day), I had a responsibility to do my job.

12 months later, I was delivering early morning papers, 6 days per week to 100 or more homes and businesses. Starting at 5:30 am, I did not have the luxury of ignoring the alarm, rolling over in my bed and going back to sleep, because my boss relied on me. Because his customers relied on him to ensure the delivery of their newspaper.

12 months on, and I was now selling newspapers to drivers of cars on their way to work, walking up and down the road, among the cars, seeing my regulars, serving them, so that when they got to work, they had the paper to read. My start time was now 4:30 am...... I would finish at 7:00 am, count the money, hand it to my boss and then ride my bike home, shower, walk to school and officially start my day, as the teachers would call it.

Why am telling you this? Because at a very young age, I got to learn that, responsibility does not always come without sacrifice. I never slept in....... by the time I got to school, I was halfway through a day's work.

I also don't want to bore you to death, with a bland tome that gathers dust on the shelf. So, there are some stories from my career, about funny stuff that has happened, some of the people I have, worked for and with and then seemingly random encounters, that have had a profound effect, sometimes fleeting and many long lasting.

It is said that art mimics life…

Not everything in life and business operates on a linear plane. This book, is not meant to be read from start to finish, it is meant to be used, as a reference source.

Whilst I have written it for people, who are in business for themselves, most, if not all of these tips, will apply to the career that you may be in, whether it be as a team leader, a teacher, a carpenter a plumber or a cleaner.

Sure, there are some lessons to be learned and some tips, to help you avoid, some of the more painful parts of being in business.

Most of all, I hope that this book is used, as a quick reference point, when you need it, a bit like a dictionary or a thesaurus is, or at least was until Google came along.

Congratulations on the Journey you are on, may it be fun, exhilarating and fulfilling.

Keep your eyes on your prize and never stop believing.

Ross Mitchell

ROSS S MITCHELL

Testimonials

Ross Mitchell you are a legend. You helped me achieve so much through your coaching. I was all over the place, you caused me and my team to focus, and hone our direction forward like no one else has ever been able too.

Most of what I enjoy today is because of your incredible skill, and no nonsense approach to identifying the business issues that needed attention and a process you help us build solutions.

I want to read your book, and pay for it.

Ross you are already a success, your book will just be an extension of your success.
Best Wishes Ken Muston

A broad thinker that articulates the English/Australian Vernacular as good as anyone
Thrives on Challenges
Damian McNamara

ROSS S MITCHELL

4 is for

4 legs to the table of success

        Passion - Love It   Vision – See It
        Commitment – Feel It   Consistency – Be It

This is a concept that I firmly believe, are essential ingredients to build a Platform of Success on. Each of these are described in further chapters.

Consider that a table with three legs is likely to be less stable than one with 4 legs, or that if the legs are of differing lengths, it won't be as strong as one that does.

When we allow ourselves to put effort into each of these legs, then the table will allow a strong foundation.

ROSS S MITCHELL

A is for

Action

If you are not in action, you are standing still……. Think about action in business, as being like a small ball of snow, at the top of the mountain….. once it starts moving, it grows until something stops it.

As a business owner, manager, leader or team member, your job is to start the ball rolling and make sure that it keeps moving, until something stops it……. And then get it moving again.

Sometimes that means a change of direction, a pivot or just a slight adjustment

Accounting

The boring stuff that, if you don't get right, will mean that everything else you do, could be for nothing

If you don't understand the finances and nuances of accounting, at least find someone who does.

The right accountant, will help you set your business up for success, by planning for the future and understanding what you don't. A mediocre accountant will help you report on the past, just so you know the mistakes, a poor one will have done nothing for you, except cost you money.

Spend the time, to find the accountant, that best suits your needs now.
Ask your friends, neighbours, colleagues and local business network, to see who comes to you well recommended.

Just like a gold nugget, they may not be easy to find, but you should keep looking until you find the right one.

Accountability.

You need it and you need to maintain it with your people at all times.

Even if you are the only one.

As you start to hire people, hold them to account as much as possible. Remember to maintain your own accountability to them, also.

Artificial Intelligence

As much as I believe that we should write our own stuff and not use AI tools such as Chat GPT and myriad other technologies, I can appreciate that they have their place in the world.

Call me a Dinosaur if you want, but as a point of reference, other than my software predicting the end of a word I am writing, I have written every word in my own voice, in fact I have typed it all without using transcription or editing software.

AI is such a moving feast and developing at such a rapid pace that, I must confess, I have nowhere near enough knowledge to comment on, with any conviction.

When writing this last few updates, I have been bombarded with Opportunities to do a 30 day deep dive / immersion program to become an AI Guru. Whilst I know that I probably need to get up to some speed, on what AI products are available to help run a business, for now I will stick to the assistance I get in Xero (where their AI is excellent) and for undertaking some research.

Authenticity

One of the most critical attributes of being a leader in your business is authenticity. It is not far different from humility. It is the power to be vulnerable, to be empathetic, to trust and be trusted.

Awards

When starting out, the last thing you are possibly considering, is entering awards. I felt the same, until the people who had assisted my start up, insisted I enter the local business awards, after less than 6 months in Nesso.

What Happened?

I was sort of embarrassed to enter, (check out impostor syndrome further on), and did it anyway.

I entered the Whitehorse Business Group Excellence in Business Awards. I submitted the entry and included my business plan.

I received a call a week later from the Chair of the Group, Cliff Dawson, who was calling to arrange an interview. We set the date for Friday afternoon, that week. Cliff arrived, we had a coffee and a glass of red wine, over the course of 2 hours. He was a really nice guy, who in time, would become a close friend mentor, and our Accountant.

When he left that afternoon, I thought nothing more of it. The awards function was a few weeks away and I didn't plan on attending. It was going to cost a few hundred dollars, that I didn't really have spare.

telling me that I should attend the function. I took my wife Shauna, and Mum and Dad.

On the night, I thought I had no chance of winning, but as advised by my sponsor, had prepared a thank you speech "all entrants should have a speech prepared Ross" When they announced the finalists in my category, I was just pleased to be one of them.

When I won, I was absolutely stunned.

I was the Best Start Up Business in the City of Whitehorse in 2004.

Business was new, but as a result of winning, press articles and introductions, I started getting work, more enquiries and was asked to join the Board of the Business Group. I later became Deputy Chair of the Group for 7 years, MC'd close to 100 functions, became well known in the local business community and got to know most of the local councillors and State Members of Parliament, who would invite me, to all sorts of things, where business opportunities continued to generate.

The week before the function, I received a call, from my start up sponsor at the Box Hill Institute,

The Bottom Line is that had I rejected that first instruction to enter, things may have been harder, who knows? The end result, from all of that, is that I met wonderful people, got better at what I did, became a really good MC, eventually became only the 4th or 5th Hall Of Fame winner and definitely improved my bottom line.

You should too.

Awesomeness.
You have it in you and will need to continue to develop yourself and your people to capitalise on it. There is an old saying that success is 1% inspiration and 99% perspiration. It is the 1% in you that you need to muster more and more as your grow.

Be prepared to invest in you and your awesomeness. Read Biographies of the successful and sometimes not so successful, meet people, be prepared to share your own stories and fallibilities, find out what makes them tick. Then choose what you do next.

B is for

Big WHY?

Your Big WHY, otherwise known as What do I DO and Why do I DO it?

If you don't know your Big Why, how can anyone, be expected to embrace you and buy from you?

If you are struggling with finding what your Big WHY is, get help.

Once upon a time I used to get people to undertake a Vision session on their own. I asked them to find a happy place, somewhere they could be alone (usually), often in nature, somewhere that they would have their natural creativity be accessible.

I used to suggest that they go to Studley Park Boathouse down by the Yarra River in Melbourne. It is only 3 kilometres from the CBD but feels like a thousand miles from nowhere. The instruction was to take $10 with them. At the time they could have got a coffee for about $3. One coffee was never enough to do the work.

They had to take a scrap book (top 2/3rds of the page are blank, bottom 1/3rd Lined) with them and a couple of pens or pencils.

Shoes off, sit on the grass, maybe dangle your feet in the water, anyway you do it, you need to be grounded.

Open the scrap book to the middle and then draw a mind map of their life. Areas to consider, Family, Fun, Finance, Career, Retirement, Legacy, Community and the middle of that, the Big WHY

Invariably people worked out their Big WHY, and that meant that their business could flourish, sometimes they worked out that they only wanted clarity about their career and left it at that.

If you are going to do this exercise today (2025) you better take $20! Coffees in Australia under $5 are hard to find

Business books.

Learn to love them, take what you need from them. Every one of them will be chocked full of good ideas. Some books, if not all don't need to be read from cover to cover. Your job is to make like an 1850's gold prospector and find the pieces you need at the time you need them.

You can always go back to the book.

A couple of my favourites…… Covey; Seven Habits, Dale Carnegie; How to Win Friends, Frankl; Man's search for meaning.

Mostly there are no bad books, Choose books that work for you.

Business Plan

You have no doubt heard the saying that "no one plans to fail, they fail to plan"

Every business needs a Business Plan. It does not need to be War and Peace!. (a 19th Century book by Tolstoy running at 1300+ pages long)

What it needs to do is set out objectives, outcomes, what, where, when, why, how, how much you will sell and how much you expect to make from selling it.

It may be complex and long, it may be simple and fit onto one page.

It needs to be concise, well thought out and most importantly followed, reviewed and reassessed regularly.

Many a business plan has been written in a very long and detailed manner only to be used as a monitor stand later on.

The best plan will be the one that works for you.

There is much debate about what a business plan should look like.

Example 1

Many years ago, I was asked to write a business plan for a company, I asked them how many pages they thought it should be………. Their reply was 100 or more…………. Why, 100 pages and what would be the value in that? was what I asked them. No real reason, they just thought the more pages the better the plan.

What I did with that client was to assist them to think about what they wanted to do, where they wanted to get to and how they wanted to do it.

We ended up with a 20 page document that could be used to describe the business, its objectives, and who it would impact. It was strategically focused; outcomes driven and could generate interest from the banks and for attracting prospective clients and employees.

It also had a one-page summary of activity that would occur over the next 12 months.

Example 2

In another example, I did a personal development program and while doing it, met a business owner from a regional area of Victoria. He found out what I did and asked if I could provide him a business plan template... " Of course I could" was my response and then I asked if he had ever had a business plan, to which he replied, he had.

Based on that reply, I asked what value was a different business plan template going to provide?

This is a very smart man, a very successful business owner. He had all the necessary tools at his disposal, a good team, a good group of advisers. What he did not have though, was someone in his business life who would ask the tough questions, someone who had no personal interest in saying yes, rather than no.

I offered to spend a half day with him and his exec team.

Asking tough questions, working out key issues and responses to those issues, we wrote them on his glass partitions in his office. Not hidden from view in a drawer like most business plans, his business plan was available for his team to see when they went to his office, on show to friends who would visit him and occasional customers who would sit in his office. This was no secret mission. It was there to be seen, to be challenged and to be a living breathing element.

This plan stayed on his partition glass for more than 12 months until it was all completed.

Needless to say, he never asked for a template ever again.

He and his team lived business planning from that day forward.

There are thousands of business plan templates available online and each has its own strengths and weaknesses. What each has, is a need to be modified to suit the person putting the plan together.

Your business plan should be YOUR Business Plan. Your pathway, your roadmap and your own style.

Take a template and modify it to suit your business or idea. Build one that means that you are immediately In Action……. If it can't be put into action, use it as a monitor stand, because that is all it is really worth and all you will ever do with it.

Brainstorming.

You are not the only one with good ideas.

Two heads are usually better than one.

If you brainstorm frequently, with your team, see what happens next. Do it anywhere, anytime and anyhow. Just do it. Have someone take notes or record the conversation on a phone or use transcription software.

I have found over the years that nuggets of gold come at the least expected time. If someone says, "can you repeat that?" often that nugget is gone it is gone forever. That is why a recording is good.

Other ways to do this is to make sure that you have anything handy to write on. Restaurants have napkins, airports have notebooks and printers in offices always have a an A4 sheet of paper or two in them. I often grab an A4 sheet and fold it in half like a book. That way I have 4 sides for multiple ideas to collect.

Once you are done, scan with your phone and share to your team, save that scan on your data system somewhere.

Branding

Who you are and what you stand for are everything in business. But what about branding, isn't that just a BIG business thingy?

Maybe, Maybe Not.

Imagine if the founders of Nike, Puma and Adidas had started Knight Sports Shoes, or Rudolf Dassler Sports Shoes, or Adolf Dassler Sports Shoes what would that have been like?

Instead, they elected to brand their shoes and their business and now look at them. 3 of the most recognisable brands globally.

Just because you are starting out doesn't mean that you need to start as Mary Jane Shoes. Branding is everything, your look, feel, interactions that people will have, how they feel when doing it.

You can too. Just take time to think it through, have it mean something or at least have a story that people can grab.

ROSS S MITCHELL

ALPHABITE SOUP FOR BUSINESS

C is for

Covid 19

In late 2019, in a far flung city in China, something weird happened. I don't know if anyone will really ever know what started a savage ball rolling.

But what transpired was something that few people could have anticipated, the world drastically altered course, it was almost as though the globe shifted on its axis.

A global Pandemic was declared.

5 years later, this virus is still around, albeit in a manner that has far less impact than in its first 18 months, where hundreds of thousands of people died, often painfully and almost always alone from their family. People were locked in their homes (some even had their doors welded shut), locked out of their countries, locked in their suburbs,
locked out of their states and left to flounder.

Countries were in dispute, airlines grounded and everything as we knew it stopped.

Companies were forced to PIVOT, to operate in a way that they had never considered, or if they had considered, had never really consented to, let alone embrace. Many closed their doors, never to open again.

Working From Home became the new norm, cities became ghost towns, Video conferencing, previously only used by major companies, was now used by everyone, Zoom flourished, with families using it, to connect with each other mere suburbs away, as people were blocked from traveling more than 5 kilometres.

Suddenly, we all needed a video conferencing pack. Microphone, Camera and fancy backgrounds. "Can you hear me?" "Turn on your mic Ross", "nice background Joanie, looks like the Amalfi Coast" became the norm in business meetings.

It was tragic and for kids, school lessons were being done online, mental health suffered then and still does today.

But what did we learn? Apart from the fact that we all found our favourite streaming services, we learned how to explore our suburbs on foot and companies found a way to do business differently. The previous reluctance of companies, to allow people to work from home, mostly out of concern that people could not be trusted to do all of their work away from the office, had to be accepted. The proof of the pudding, would be in the eating, and a fine pudding most people found they were eating.

Then it became evident that an upshot for a company with lots of employees and lots of leased commercial real estate space, that working from home would allow companies to save money on rent, staff amenities and improve their bottom line, or at least stop the bleeding, which resulted from a near cessation of business.

Staff were required to commute less, some working longer, some working more effectively, some loving, it some hating it, some finding it better for their family lifestyle.

The reality, is the pandemic provided a reset for many people, forced? yes, necessary?, probably begrudgingly? yes and accepted by many and others with open arms.

Ultimately, one of the things, that came out of this awful event, is that people found that they have more options than ever.

What we eventually end up with, as the "Normal" way of doing business, is still unknown. It may be, that the great majority of people end up working a hybrid model, of WFH 2 or 3 days per week and the balance in an Office, seems to be the consensus of most people.

Despite what many employees feel that it is better for them to have a hybrid, there are many commentators and politicians, who insist that a return to the office, full time, is what is required to refresh and rejuvenate, desolate Central Business Districts and suburban / regional business centres.

Then there are people, who are the engine of the economy, Small Business owners. The ones I speak to, are on the fence, about what is ultimately best. They like that they have a lesser requirement for leased space and the associated cost savings, while lamenting the reduction in collaboration, that occurs, when teams are in close proximity to each other. Let's call that the "water cooler effect", for want of a term.

What can business learn? Be open to opportunities, otherwise opportunities will continue to pass your door. How you did business yesterday, is unlikely to be how will do business in 5 years' time, maybe even tomorrow.

Capitalise

On your ideas, your experience and your surroundings. In a post Covid19 world, be bold, daring and decisive.

Make your own running, create a business plan. It can be brief, it can be on the back of an envelope, on a serviette or on a mirror or window.

Be like the Nike slogan…….. JUST DO IT

Capital

Capital of the working kind is what you will need.

Yes, every good idea can be used to start a business, but being under resourced can hinder you at the start, the middle and may ultimately spell the end.

Many a potentially great business has fallen over for lack of money. If you are really certain of your idea, you may access equity from your own home (comes with risk and will place stress on you), from family and friends (comes with stress and has been known to end relationships), from venture capitalists (if you can secure a VC, you will no doubt be sacrificing either ownership, high repayments or both) or any other source you can find.

From a personal perspective, I can safely say that a lack of available working capital meant that from day 1, I was under constant pressure to produce a result.

To put that into context, I effectively made a decision, to leave paid employment, without lining up my financial ducks. I was blissfully unaware of, just how much the self-employed are like pariahs to money lenders. Had I known then, what I knew a few weeks later, I would have gone from having a standard mortgage, to applying for and gaining a line of credit facility on my home loan. That would have at least provided me a bit of a buffer and some much needed emotional respite that comes from having to come up with mortgage payments, during start-up phase while not really earning. It still remains one of my greatest regrets and could have been solved, through being more patient, in wanting to "hang out my shingle"

The best advice that I could offer, in this respect, is that however much money, you think you will need to get started, increase that amount by at least double. The stress of being under resourced can be overwhelming.
Capital of the intellectual kind will only get you so far.

After that, hard work, resilience, smart marketing and good delivery is essential

You need to know the value of your Intellectual Capital and understand that it doesn't need to be your formal education, and it might be. What it will be, is the cumulative result of your education, your lived and learned experiences, your family, your connections, your shortcomings, your exceptional qualities and your environment.

Whatever the perceived value of your intellectual capital, it should not stop you. What will stop you, is you. (refer to the intro to know where I am coming from)

Cash is NOT Profit

Just as profit doesn't always translate to cash, cash is not profit.

The cash that you have, is something that you are managing, on behalf of a myriad of people and bodies.

At any point, you will be holding Tax Payable, money owed to suppliers and other creditors, staff, superannuation, lease payments.

It is true, that your bank balance may be great, but you may not be making any profit.

Read further about Margin and Mark Up to gain an insight into why

Cashflow Forecast

If you don't run your cash it will run you!. ....Huh I hear you say.

Cash is not always folding stuff, in fact today, with an almost cashless society, it is almost never folding stuff.

It is the health of your bank balance, the ability to pay your bills as and when they fall due (insolvency is when you can't).

Don't mistake Profit For Cash….. more on that later in Profit.

Knowing when Money is coming in and going out, is what cashflow is. It needs to be understood and needs to be managed.

It is the stuff that matters.

There are lots of cashflow templates you can use from Excel or your Accounting software package.

Coach or no coach

When you start your business, there are so many things you need to know. The reality is that you cannot know everything you need to know.

In all probability, you will not be able to afford to hire everyone you need, to do the things you know you don't know how to do. That doesn't even cover the things you don't even know, you don't know.

The reality is that, a coach will stand with you, for you and occasionally against you, so that you take actions, for yourself and your business that you may want to avoid and are necessary for you to succeed.

As a coach, I always had a coach. To do anything less, would be disingenuous.

> ### Example
> I had a client who used to come to events, I was holding.
> He came so that he could be my "Intro Guy"
> He was very passionate about business, life, family, planes, cars and everything he came across.
> His intro would go like this.

"Hi I'm Ken Muston, I sell cars.

Have you ever heard of Ian Thorpe?, He is the best swimmer in the world.

Do you think he got that way because he jumped in the pool and started swimming, or because he had a perfect stroke and already knew what to do to become the best swimmer in the world? Of course he didn't.

He became the best swimmer in the world because he had a great coach.

So why is it, that business people expect to open the doors, hang a shingle out and have the best business without a coach?"

It's crazy.

You are about to hear from Ross Mitchell, he is Australia's best business coach and you should listen, because he makes business easier, because he looks at your business from the outside and has you do things you have not even thought of. ...."

I worked with Ken and his team for more than 6 years. There were tears, triumphs, droughts and great times, and he has written a testimonial at the front of the book

Commitment

The 3rd of the 4 Legs to the Table of Success. This is the stickability factor.

What are you committed to? Is it because of the money and needing to make the mortgage payments? Is that you have burnt the bridge so you cannot retreat?

Sun Tzu in his book "Art of War" taught armies to burn their boats and destroy the bridges behind them, as they advanced into new territory. He argued that soldiers without the option of taking flight, are more likely to prevail, over their objective.

When you are committed to the outcome and do what is necessary, you are more likely to achieve success.

Complaints

They are similar to criticism. But unlike criticism (mostly an opinion), complaints are mostly realistic and often very uncomfortable to hear and if ignored, or dismissed as frivolous or even vexatious, will cost you and your business dearly.

What must be remembered about complaints, is that like a good service or product, few if any people complain to YOU about YOUR service or product. They say 1 out of 10 people tell their friends about good service, but 9 out of 10 will tell their friends about bad service.

Which means, when someone complains, they at least feel you deserve a chance to redeem yourself.

Complaints give you gold. They give you the chance to review, revisit and improve.

Ignore complaints at your peril.

Commercial Terms

Can you walk into a supermarket and help yourself to your week's groceries, without paying for them? Same for a hotel stay, a flight on a plane, lunch or dinner at a café or restaurant? Of course not? Is it because you would be embarrassed to walk out without paying, or because you already know what is expected, agreed or implied?

Just as the supermarket, café airline and hotel have rules, so should you, if you expect payment, for your product or service.

Without stating the bleeding obvious, it is essential that you have a set of clearly stated Commercial Terms, for doing business between yourself and your customers.

At the very least your Commercial Terms should state:
- What you will do for the customer
- What you won't do

- What you will charge extra for
- When payment is due—**Please note that unless you are a bank, do not finance your customer's business by generous terms. A customer who pays you slow is not a great customer**
- What happens if payment is not made by your customer? **Penalties are applied, by the various State and Federal Tax Offices all the time, for late payment and lodgement. So should you. Look up Tax office rates and apply them into your commercial terms.**

Importantly, in relation to the Commercial Terms you set with your customers, you will get the customers and cash flow that you deserve, based on what is set out in your terms and how well you apply them.

Good terms that are clear, fair, understood and applied, as and when they should be, will work for you and your customers.

If they lack one or more of those ingredients, you will have problems collecting cash. And that will eventually end your venture .

Condemn

Dale Carnegie says that "you should never Criticise, Condemn or Complain".

By condemning a person, you are creating a barrier, for that person and their ability to be a contribution to you, your business and your customers.

If you need to provide feedback to someone, do so in a manner that allows them to feel empowered, to do something about it, to take appropriate action, to retain their dignity.

Consistency

The 4th leg of the Table of Success is as important as anything you do

Consistent effort, will produce consistent results, good or bad, so you will want to make sure that the efforts you put in, are of a consistent standard and consistently refined, to ensure that what you are doing is producing what you are wanting.

Tying your effort to results, through measuring the appropriate markers, is essential.

Criticism

Depending on where it is coming from, it may cause you to sink or swim.

Here is the thing, criticism is someone's opinion and opinions are like bums, everyone has one and they believe theirs to be right. It doesn't mean it is, and it may be.

I have a saying that "the last perfect person had a really bad Good Friday", so be sure of this. Criticism will, eventually, come your way……. simply put, it is not preventable.

How you respond to the criticism, is up to you. You may choose to listen or not, you can be like a matador, allow the criticism to pass by, say thanks and move on, or you may elect to stand, in front of the bull and get skewered by the bull's horns.

If the criticism is internal (the noisy voice on your shoulder), listen to it, say thanks and then tell it get the hell out of your way. It will still be there, no matter what you are doing, it will always want to run the show…… it's up to you how you handle it and whether you let it run you or you run it..

If you need to criticise someone, do so in private.

If you want to give praise, do so in public!

ROSS S MITCHELL

D is for

Data management & protection

Your business, any business relies on Data, whether it be to run inventory, your accounting system, your client records, your HR and Payroll system and myriad other systems.

So what? I hear you say, that is so obvious.

Yes it probably is.

So if something is very important, what are the fundamentals?

Protection of, or the security and privacy of that data (you definitely do not want to be THAT company, who releases personal info into the ether).

Protection of the Intellectual Property, that you have built over time.

Protection of access to the data via firewalls, or cloud access.

How about, just plain common sense around password protection, to everything you own or need access to.

A quick question for you.

Do you have a Use of Technology Policy, that applies equally to everyone in your business, including yourself, your family, your staff and any contractors who has access to your system? If so, has each person signed it and held on your records.

How many passwords do you have, that are the same? How many apps do you have on your system, that are not approved by your IT dude? How many two factor identifications have you got turned on? All of them or just some? Is Bio Metric access on, at every opportunity?

How many of your staff have access to each other's accounts, because they share their passwords and access points?

If you have local storage of your data system, is it backed up daily? Where is the backup stored?

Do you have a UPS: Uninterruptible Power Supply, to handle shutting down your IT system securely, in the event of a power failure? If so when did you last test it? Does it work?

I know that sounds like a lot to think about and it is. It is also critical to ensure that you can continue to operate.

History is littered with companies who could not recover data in the event of a major outage, fire, flood or accident.

The belief is that if you cannot restart operations within 5 days of an event, the likelihood of business failure, is increased beyond comprehension.

DO NOT RISK BEING UNDERPREPARED FOR IT.

Development

Development of the

Personal type. You need to read books, magazines, listen to audiobooks, podcasts etc. in your car, the train, the bus or ferry and if you travel, do it on a plane (read or listen).

Choose material that gets your juices flowing, it could be a really great story, about someone who inspires you, it could be about a topic that inspires you, or could be something that just allows your mind to wander. I really like a broad range of books, sports people, actors, coaches, inspirational stuff about people who have overcome adversity.

I also really enjoy action-adventure stories, with a love story embedded. (Kendall Talbot is one of my favourites)

Different genres are important to explore, to keep the mind open.

Business type takes time effort and creativity. Schedule it daily and maintain it. Understand why you are in business, what your big why is! Take no prisoners.

There is a thing I learnt from a mentor many years ago, about a thing they called "the Universal Principle of Lag".

Essentially, there is a lag of 90 days, from the start of an activity, to the time that results start to be produced.

Think about it for a moment! Just because you say you are open for business, doesn't mean that you will be noticed and grabbing customers off the street straight away. People like to see other people using that business, so that they feel confident that the business will be there when they are ready. This takes time.

It is one of the reasons that nightclubs use a spotlight on opening night and have a velvet rope and a line up on the street. The line must mean that the nightclub is the place to be right! Maybe, or it could be so that they get noticed and you stop and go inside.

You get the drift.

Business Development is essential at all times and needs to continue even when you are busy.

Example

I remember being called into the boardroom at one of my long-term employer's offices more than 20 years ago.

Present were the owners and the external Accountant / business advisor. At first I was wondering what I was doing wrong... am I about to get the bullet?

The Accountant proceeds to tell me, that the business has a looming cash flow problem, mainly because I had been winning too much high value business. He told me that I had to stop tendering, marketing and business building for 3 months. Whilst I did not have the language to explain "the Universal Principle of Lag", I instinctively knew, that if I ceased activities for 3 months, that the cashflow crisis coming would be magnified 6-9 months later, as we would have no new work coming on stream.

I fought for a shift in the approach, more sales and relationship building activities, rather than hitting the tender marketplace.

Thankfully the Managing Director agreed, although the Accountant didn't.

I did more work with my contacts, developed new ones.

Opportunities continued to come through for us, at a more profitable and sustainable basis and with greater probability of winning, than the open tender market.

Many of those relationships have been with me, through career changes and friendships endure to this day.

Discounts

Just as having commercial terms, is important for your success, so is the need to understand the impact that a discount strategy will have on your profitability.

I am dead against using discounting as an effective strategy for making sales.

A 10% discount may seem like a good thing to entice a customer, and it may well be.

Discounting can however, often lead to an expectation that the price you have now is too high, or one that you don't believe in, and could even create a belief that if I wait long enough, you will be on sale again.

A discount is money straight off your bottom line and may send you down a deathly slope.

Example

In Australia there are a group of retailers, who anyone with patience to wait, knows that they will be on sale very soon.

One of those is Rivers, a retailer originating in Ballarat Victoria some time mid to late 1970s or 1980s. I remember, as a young guy, buying Rivers shoes meant you paid full price in Melbourne, or went to the seconds outlet, on a weekend away, in Ballarat.

Rivers then, only sold shoes, they were Australian Made and of good quality.

For whatever reason, Rivers transitioned to selling a broad range of clothing. For the past 15 years, you would not go to Rivers and pay full price for anything, because you knew that it would only be 2, 3 or 4 weeks until it would be on sale at heavily discounted rates.

As at March 2025, Rivers along with its parent company, is closing its doors, millions of dollars in debt and leaving countless people without a job, both here and in manufacturing centres abroad.

Without knowing the full picture of the operations, I can't help but think that I am not the only person who stopped paying full price for their stuff.

Sometimes diversification can be a not so good thing..

DISCOUNT at your peril.

Instead, offer 10% more bonus product of something. The value perception, to the customer, of doing so, is better than having them feel that you have been ripping them off. Or worse, having them hold off buying just waiting for the discount sales period

ROSS S MITCHELL

E is for

Employees or Contractors?

As you grow you, will have the opportunity to expand your offering. This will mean, more people to do the work. You will be faced with considering, what basis do you engage them,

Do you employ the people as **direct employees,** with all of the associated responsibilities and commitments that come with that?

This includes paying them an agreed amount (Wages or Salary), often in line with an Industrial Award, Superannuation, Annual Leave, Personal leave, Workers Compensation Insurance, Payroll Tax (maybe not immediately but at some point), travel allowances, uniforms, electronic equipment (laptop, phone car etc). For arguments sake, if the person earns $40 per hour your cost to employ that person will exceed $60 per hour.

Or do you pay them as a contractor? Then they are responsible for their own Annual Leave, personal Leave and the other bits and pieces. They will often provide their own electronic equipment etc.

You will still pay that person around $60 per hour. So, what is the difference and what is the big deal?

An employee remains your ongoing concern, even when times change, even when they are not performing the way you hoped, or when they are not at work and the work is piling up, or when there is no work to be done.

A contractor's work agreement with you, will invariably be more flexible. It will mean more work for them, when you need it, less work for them, when you don't have much for them to do.

So, what you do, will be based on what you believe is best for you and the team at the time.

Either way you go, make sure that you follow the section, Hire Slowly, Fire Quickly.

Engagement

It is essential that you engage, your staff and your customers. Your family will need to be fully engaged with you and your ideas.

Business is tough enough, without having people, right there in your corner. Make sure, that you have them able to tell other people that they meet, what it is that you do. If they can't, odds are, you have not been able to articulate your business, well enough and that will mean that the people you want to sell to, will struggle to "get it" also.

Do the work, on knowing how to engage with people, from all walks of life.

If you cannot speak to people, from the C-Suite, to the Shop Floor and all points in between, you must learn to.

> I remember being told, by a couple of my team working with me back in the 2000s, that I had the "Language of a Common Man".
>
> I was furious with them, called them a pair of intellectual snobs, because I thought that were having a crack at me…. After all they had University education and diplomas on the wall. I didn't then and still don't today.
>
> When I stopped the rant, they both went on to say that they wish that they could relate to people as well as I could.

The lesson there is, be yourself, and treat everyone as an equal, in a respectful way.

F is for

Financial Freedom

At least that is possibly one reason, why you are in business.

The reality could be very different, if you don't get the Finance part right.

Financial Literacy

You need to understand your numbers, you need to love your numbers and MUST NOT NEGLECT THE NUMBERS.

You do not need to be an accountant, but there are key areas you must know intimately.

Profit and Loss, Cash Flow, EBITDA, Interest Rates, Cash Ratio, Hourly Operational Cost, the difference between Mark Up and Margin, are a few.

Use your accountant, to help you with understanding the key numbers, for your business.

Funding

Friends, family, foes maybe, and you can mostly forget about the bank for funding you.

What might seem the easiest way to keep the business financed, is to use the equity in your home. That is true up to a point.

But as Kenny Rogers sang, "you've got to know when to hold them know when to fold them"

Going back to the "well" of your property is ok, until you have been there, too many times and then all you have to show for years of work, is a much bigger mortgage, than when you started

Funding activity in a small business is tough. It is also something you should seek to do from cashflow, by having your clients fund your business. Just think for a moment, sales generate funds, no sales equals no funds……. Therefore, if there are funds from sales, your business is being funded by your clients and that should spark joy.

If you are the one funding the business all time, i.e. spending more than you are earning, you are, in reality funding your staff to live, as well as those of your clients or prospective clients.

Example

Many years ago, I joined an emerging Cleaning business who was doing healthy numbers. It was what would have been classed as a mid-tier company, owned by some really good people.

We were working with some of Australia's largest property funds.

We were sitting in the boardroom of one of the largest fund managers in the country in a Tender interview.

When it came to agreeing to the contract conditions in the tender documents, one of the conditions was to agree to 30-day payment at the end of the month. This meant 60 days terms.

The CEO says "we are a small family business and cash flow is very important to us. We really can't agree to the delayed payment terms as we must pay staff wages every 14 days. Would you consider paying us 1/26th of the contract every 14 days?"

I was floored, even embarrassed by the request as I had a good picture of the health of the business.

To my amazement the client agreed.

That preparedness to be vulnerable and real, meant that the client was now funding the business rather than the owners.

Think about your terms and how you could improve funding, without accessing Home Loan Lines Of Credit.

ROSS S MITCHELL

G is for

Gig work is Legitimate.

The way that we work has changed so far in 5 years, it is hard to fathom.

Whether you build a linear career, or single focused business, it really is up to you.

The advent of Gig Work has created opportunities for people, to live the life they want.

GIG WORK or a GIG BUSINESS, is a Legitimate way to build your life. It is not for the unemployable, or lowest paid people on the food chain.

Up until the mid-2010's, most people worked on a career, or a single business and periodically took holidays, or the occasional sabbatical. They did that for 40 or 50 years, until they retired, which meant traveling; until they got too old for travel then played golf or lawn bowls, until they died.

Sounds dumb doesn't it?

Gig Work and Gig Business brings a chance to change the narrative.

It brings choice.

What it does need you to do is, to OWN that space and set up all the other things that a business needs.

G is not for Good Fast & Cheap (GF&C)

Sometimes called the iron triangle where a client hopes to have it all. They want it now, they want it perfect, and they want it at a discount. Not happening on my watch. There is no way they can.

In year 11 economics I learnt about equilibrium, "the point at which buyers and sellers agree". Thanks Phil Reynolds.

There is no equilibrium in GF&C. You may have 2 of them, good and fast but it should never be cheap, good and cheap, but you will need to wait a while and fast and cheap will never be good.

Stick to your guns, set your price, negotiate if you must but without a margin that you can live with, you may as a well call yourself a charity When you are asked by your client to do GF&C, ask them "what they would do if they were you being asked to do what they are asking?" The answer might interest you

GOYA KOD

What the Heck? That is almost what I said, when I recently read a book, "The Strangler" so this is definitely not an original idea.

When I first saw the words GOYA KOD written in the book it made we wonder what on earth was the significance, until in the last few pages it was revealed.

A journo had this on her typewriter (pre 1990 that was what people used before computers).

As a journo, she had this stuck on her typewriter, to remind herself every day, what she must do.

If you are reading this as a Sales Dude, or any other business owner, you must do this also.

Hope you are ready for it.

Get Off Your Ar.. and Knock On Doors.

Greatness

It is your greatness that has you branch out into business. Congratulate yourself, build on it and make it your strength.

H is for

Helicopters

Taking a helicopter view of your business, on a weekly basis, is essential to keeping things moving.

The overall strategy will be formed at 30,000 feet, where you can see the start and the end. That is essential, but operating at that height, will not allow you to see the minutiae that creates the problems or gives you the immediate results.

Hire Slowly Fire Quickly

I worked with a mentor for 10 years and she would actively promote the concept that, People are Hired for their skill and Fired for their Attitude.

Put simply, the great sales dude may be great at sales, and has a terrible attitude, that didn't show up in the 2, 20 minute interviews you did, and the referees they gave you, are the ones that never saw the real them, or maybe just pleased to see the back of them.

Hiring the wrong person, or people can be a Culture Killer, so **Hire Slowly**

As much as you may feel that you need more people, take the time, to find the RIGHT people, YOUR people.

When you realise that the person, you Hired in a Hurry, is not right for the business, Fire Quickly. It may not be easy, but trust me, it will not get any easier the longer that you tolerate their behaviours, or do your business reputational damage.

Honesty

Make no mistake, Honesty is everything, even when it is uncomfortable.

Be honest with yourself, to your friends and family.

Having to face up to reality and addressing the elephant in the room, is a critical success factor. Avoidance, rarely benefits anyone.

If business is not going well, faking it may be necessary for a while, but lying about stuff, will do more harm than good, in the long term

Having an honest and critical conversation, with a team member about their performance, will be beneficial, to both you and they, when you have it.

Human Resources

You have probably encountered the HR department, at some point, often times it is not a fun experience.

How you set up your business, when it comes to HR, depends on what type of business you have.

It is Your job for You to set policy and theirs to enact it

My tip is, that you allow the HR team to do what you NEED them to. Do, not what they want you to do unless is to keep your business safe

Skilled HR Professionals, can be your best ally in business, protecting you from making poor hiring decisions, setting up good and robust policies for employment, and termination, for when you have to make those tough calls.

Just as a much as a skilled HR professional can be your ally, the wrong HR team, can make your life miserable, by applying the handbrake to your success.

Find HR support, by asking around, use a consultant if you don't think your business is big enough to warrant a fulltime employee. That way, you can test whether you need to keep the system going.

Humility

Being Humble is not being weak, in fact, if anything, it is being courageous and requiring the capacity for vulnerability.

When, for all your life, you have been in a contest, that says "only the fittest survive", "for me to win you must lose", it takes something extraordinary to put your hand up and say, I messed up, I don't know, I don't understand.

We all know narcissists and know how little they share of themselves; how much they believe, that they are the centre of the universe and that, everyone else around them, is just there to serve them. They always believe that they have the answer and that they are smarter than everyone else. They love taking credit for success and shoving blame on others when failure has occurred.

I would rather be someone who is prepared to say, "I don't know" than make up some rubbish on the run.

Example

I worked for a company, many moons ago.

I had only recently joined them and was asked to tender for a major cleaning contract, out in Western Queensland, a large mining company.

If you have ever understood anything about Mining, the most important agenda item, is always safety, then safety, then safety.

My boss and I were at the pitch meeting / tender interview. Prior to going into the meeting, I said to him that we should sit side by side, so that if one of us talked too much, or was saying dumb stuff, we could give a quick tap on the ankle and shut it down. Unfortunately, my boss sat 2 seats away, on the very large, boardroom table.

We had been going really well, and the interview was almost wrapped up. Thanks, had been exchanged and I was confident, that we had done enough, to win the contract.

The client then said "one more question. What are your LTIs?"

If you don't know what they are, LTIs are Lost Time Injuries…… a very, very important indicator in the mining sector.

As I had only been with the business a short while, I wasn't sure and said, "I am not sure, but I will get back to you with the Frequency and Severity Rate by 5 pm today". Client happy, we bought time.

My boss the narcissist says, "what are LTIs?"

Client exasperatingly says "Lost Time Injuries" Boss says "Pretty Good, we don't have many"

Client opens file and ceremoniously strikes through his notes with a big X, says "that will be all fellas"

We were officially dead to them.

Moral of the story, if you don't know the answer, admit it and assure the person that you will find out.

ALPHABITE SOUP FOR BUSINESS

I is for

"IF IT IS TO BE IT IS UP TO ME"
-Unknown

Identity theft insurance

A new thing. It won't happen to me; I am too small to be a target... Those sneaky emails, texts, that innocent click of the mouse while you are distracted. That is all it takes

If you knew the hassles and time involved to recover your identity in the event that it is stolen, you would be insane not to protect it wouldn't you?

It takes experts between 80-100 hours to recover your identity. You will take even longer.

While you are doing that, what is happening to your business?

The best thing, is that you can now insure yourself for, what amounts to an insignificant amount of money, every year.

If you would like to know more about how you can protect your identity, send an email to me personally and I can help point you to a product, from Norton.

Independence

There is no **I** in team.

Very true. But there are times when as the business owner, creator and funder, you are the only one who can make a call.

Just make sure that when you do so, you do it with the full facts.

Information Technology

This area continues to defy all sense.

The smartphone in your hand your pocket or on the desk has more power than the computers used to send man to the moon in 1969. Talk about "One Small Step for Man and One Giant Leap for Mankind"

Today, you can create an invoice and take payments on your smartphone, so that you speed up how quickly you are paid. See Funding to understand why this is important.

Printers are networked and can print wi-fi. Not sure if you will need a printer, but it can happen, nonetheless.

The software you need to operate can be effectively hired for small change, compared to having a downloaded system specific software, that might cost thousands of dollars.

Your investment into IT will depend on what you are doing. For the majority of people, a Smartphone, Laptop and Tablet are all you need to operate.

When you are doing something bigger, that might involve building a team of people, or a retail business you will probably need more than that.

The smart money is, seek out advice on what you need, engage a smart IT Dude who can understand what your business is about and can help you build a scalable platform to launch from.

Innovation

It is easy to think that innovation, is something that only an expert can do. You will no doubt, be faced with a need to improve something in your business, along the way. It may be that you need to tip everything out on the floor and sift through the pile to find the corner pieces, or a may just be a simple tweak.

Either way, you will need to confront the issue.

What you need to understand is, Innovation is not something that is only for the experts, it is for you. I believe that to be an expert in something, can lead you to a lack of innovation.

I recently watched an interview with Simon Goodwin, an AFL Football coach. He was on the way home from a bad loss, when his son said to him that, he needed to play a player completely out of position, the next week. He could have dismissed that opinion and kept doing the same thing over and over (definition of insanity). He didn't, he made the change and from that point forward, they won every game, including the premiership.

Is that innovation or is that just luck? Doesn't really matter, it was a tweak, an improvement in the process and delivered a different result. I would say that is Innovation.

If you are an expert in your business, approach it with restless discontent and seek to innovate every day. Equally importantly, be open to ideas from the outside. You might just win YOUR premiership.

Insurance

You insure your car, your home, your contents, don't you?

You may have private health insurance. Personally, I reckon that Private Health Insurance is essential for business owners. Another time for that though.

Example

In 2018, I was involved in a serious Motorcycle accident and have not really worked in a full capacity since then, so I know from personal experience the importance of these.

Frankly without them I would not have been able to survive financially over the last few years.

When it comes to Insurance for you and your business, there are non-negotiables.

You SHOULD consider the following:
- Income Protection Insurance
- Trauma / Crisis Recovery Insurance
- Life/ Total and Permanent Disability Insurance (TPD)

You MUST Have the following:
- Products Liability Insurance
- Professional Indemnity Insurance
- Public Liability Insurance

Find an insurance broker to work with. It seems expensive at the time and is, but God forbid, and you have an accident, or significant illness that stops you from being able to work at your normal capacity or fully, at the time when you are in greatest need, and you have to make a claim, you will be grateful that you made some sacrifices along the way.

Integrity

Let me be clear about this. "You are nothing without your integrity"

Integrity is doing the hard things, when there is an easier way, that lacks accountability

Integrity is following up, when you said you would. It is doing the right thing, when doing the wrong thing right, might seem like a good option.

Only you can set the agenda of your integrity and only you, will really know when you have missed the boat in being integrous

J is for

Jumping out of your skin

If you are not jumping out of your skin at least once a day, then you maybe should question why you are putting yourself and your family through all of this.

Journey of a lifetime

Whether the journey of a lifetime is because it was everything you wanted it to be, or the one you remember as an unmitigated disaster, will come down to several factors.

To avoid the disaster, research, plan, think, decide, act, plan, think decide, plan, act, refresh, reinvigorate, research, development and plan, research, act, build, plan, act, act, act, act, plan, review, reassess, act plan ....And when you think you are done, repeat.

ROSS S MITCHELL

K is for

Key Performance Indicators

"If it counts it can be counted and just because it can be counted doesn't mean it counts!"

KPIs are the stats that matter, and you will need these for every facet of your business. They should become as familiar to you, as the dashboard in your car.

Which KPIs you decide are right for your business, will be up to you and your shareholders (initially your family, or if you are single your pet)

Good KPIs for all business include, Profitability, cash in bank (which is definitely not profit), sales volume, average customer spend, hourly operating cost, labour to sales ratio, COGS (cost of goods sold)

Whatever you decide upon, keep the list as short as possible and as long as necessary, all the while giving you complete control

ROSS S MITCHELL

L is for

Lag Time

Just because you open the doors today, may not mean that you will make a sale tomorrow, or for that matter be able, to deliver a product.

Lag is the thing that scuppers many people's plans, when they don't make a sale right away.

The universal principle of lag, for a service business is that it takes about 90 days to activate a client from first activity to purchase.

Unless you can activate every prospect, you identify, you need to have a very big pipeline

Love

Love is an underused word when it comes to business. Why? Is it because it shows weakness, is too soppy, or should only be used for matters of the heart?

Well, if you don't love your business, your clients, your staff (not in a sexual way), then your business will, invariably be transactional and subject to a range of competitive pressures, that could otherwise be avoidable.

Think about how hard it could be, getting out of bed each day if you did not love your business… you could be miserable, and your

staff and customers will feel it. They will realise that there are options aplenty. Transactional!

If you don't love your clients, they will feel it and move on, again transactional.

If you don't love your staff, they will feel it and move on, again transactional.

Do you know what that costs?

Customer Acquisition is infinitely more difficult, than retention. Current clients already know how to work with you, just as you know how to work with them. Getting to know new customers' habits and expectations, takes time and costs a lot of money.

Talent Acquisition is hugely expensive, just taking into account recruitment costs alone, without considering how long it takes to train the new person, into YOUR way of doing things. Then there is the loss of knowledge from the business, the potential for that Good, but disgruntled, employee to join a competitor. They may even be able to coerce that customer base,(the base that they have shown love to),to join them, at their new company.

And all of that, because you were not prepared to show some love.

M is for

Margin versus Mark-up

I first learned the difference between Margin and Mark Up, as a 19 year-old at Kmart and that still remains, if not THE most important business lesson of my life, it is definitely top 3. Thanks Len Colliss.

Margin is what is left over for you, when you make the sale (Profit)

People speak about Gross Profit (GP). That is, when something sells for $100 and costs $60 to buy and Sell. The Gross Profit is $40. Or 40% GP

Now if we reversed that and said, what we are selling costs $60 and we want to sell it for $100, our mark-up is $40. Or 66.66%.

How can one figure be 40% and the other be 66.6%, even though the dollars are the same, but the percentages are very different and why does it matter?

Why it matters, is that most people understand their costs, as that is the starting point of a sale. It may be one hour's labour or one widget.

You know something costs $60 but don't know how much you should sell it for, but you know that you need to get a margin of 40%.

If margin and mark up are the same thing, let's just use margin of 40%. We add 40% onto $60 and we now have $84. That is $16 less than what is needed and only 30% GP

Example

I worked with a client, several years ago, who insisted that he had a trading margin (GP) of 37% and could not make profit. In my years of business, 37% GP is pretty good, and in his sector, would have been at the better end.

I was miffed.

When I asked him what his mark-up was, he said 37%. I said to him that if his mark-up was 37%, his margin could not be.

He was certain he was right, and I was wrong until I showed the example above.

He needed to have a mark-up of 50% on every sale to achieve his 37% Margin.

He did that and over time he recovered his lost margin.

YOU MUST UNDERSTAND YOUR TRUE COSTS AND REALLY LOVE YOUR NUMBERS

Money

If you are not in it for the money, then what are you in it for?

I have heard many people say that "I don't do it for the money". What you need to be able to say is that "I would do it for free". When you can say that, then you are doing it for the right reasons. Let's be clear though, that if it is not the money, go and do some volunteer work and find the thing, that is about the money.

If it is because you already have heaps of money, support a charity, or support a young person, to give them a chance in starting a business.

N is for

Never Say Never

Never is a long time!

I will never take on that work, I would never sell my service or product at that low a price, I would never use an offshore workforce, etc.

Until you have been around a while and seen what other people are doing, what they are making work and experiencing, why would you close your mind to possibility. There are some amazing things to be experienced out in the world and if you say never, how can you expect to experience them.

Just think what cars would be like if Henry Ford had taken the early advice of his engineers, saying that a v8 engine could not be built

Rather than saying "I could never do that", try, "what would happen if I did. ?"

NO

Learn to love the word NO.

Learn to love saying it, hearing it and doing NOthing. Contrary to popular belief NO is very powerful.

When you say it, you get to have a void. When a glass is full, there is no more room in it, so you have to be able to tip some of the liquid out to be able to put something in. If it is full, of all the same thing and someone, or something, more flavoursome comes along, you have no room for it. The void allows for additional experiences

When you hear the word NO, during a sales call, celebrate. The fact that you heard NO, means that you were doing something and are getting closer to a YES. Read the book "Going For No"

Doing NOthing, means that you are having a break. It is essential to plan regular breaks, in your day, your week, your month and year. Remember, all work and no play makes Johnny a very dull boy

NO means no, now, not never

Sales rejection hurts, if you let it.

When someone says No, say "thanks". Be humble

And then ask the next question, is there a better time to approach this? Does that mean never? Or you could choose an open-ended question. What would be the best time to approach this in the future?

Or you could be very courageous and ask whether it is because the product or YOU don't suit them?

O is for

"if you are not open to opportunity, it will continue to pass your door"- Ross Mitchell

Opportunity

There are opportunities everywhere you look.

You just have to know, which ones are ideas and which ones are opportunities.

Have a process to decide which ones are right for YOU because they fit with your plan, your strategy and values.

Stay true to the plan, assess whether that opportunity is one that is right for you, or whether it is going to be a distraction, that will prevent you from achieving your greatness.

Office

Office space can be expensive, it can be cheap, it can be a home office, it could be a serviced office, it could be a shared office.

In 2025, there is no right or wrong answer.

Which type you have will depend on what you are doing, how many people you have working for you, who comes to see you and what message / image do you wish to portray to yourself, your staff, your customers and competitors

Example

When I first started coaching and consulting, I worked out of a small study at home. I grew a bit and started having more and more coaching sessions with clients. The lack of privacy (and a whiteboard) in coffee shops was not very good for that. I also really wanted to optimise my time, so traveling to customers, was not something that excited me, nor made commercial sense.

At that time, serviced offices were not really a thing, so a commercial office rent of $30- $50K, was even less appealing than coffee shops.

At Easter, in 2004, I decided to convert half my garage into an office, so I went and bought some materials, and built an office inside my garage. Over the next few years as business grew and I had staff and associates coming to work from home, I took over the whole garage.

The space was functional and could accommodate 6 people at desks. The meeting/ coaching room overlooked my courtyard garden and was very private.

In the 10 years I worked from home, only once did a client feel it inappropriate and never came there again.

I wonder whether that client would have said the same if it was today, where most of us have experienced working from home with many people never wanting to "go to the office again"

Which way you go, make the decision that is right for you.

P is for

Passion

The 1st of the 4 legs to the table of success.

Passion is loving what you do, doing something for money, even though you would do it for free. Something that has you jumping out of your skin.

People ask me, why I do what I do? Why coach, Why write, Why impart wisdom?

Simple, I like to think, that people who read this work, or hear me speak, will take just something from it and be better at what they do, or get better results from what they do.

I love people, I like to help people.

Being your best every day, takes work and when you are passionate about that work, then work is easier.

People

People who need people, are the happiest people!

Actually, people who work with people and experience success together, are the happiest people

Rarely do your staff "rip you off", most people are good natured, good hearted and warm. If you keep them informed, about why things are happening, they don't have to invent, in their heads, what is going on. If times are tough, let them know, if the vision is changing, let them know, if you have a new idea, test it with them.

Trust is a two-way street! Someone has to start the process of trust, and that person looked at you this morning when you brushed your teeth.

Perseverance and Persistence

Being persistent and perseverant are essential ingredients. Having these 2 interchangeable qualities will help you through and to avoid the tough times.

It is easy to give up, so it is necessary to stay strong

When you are selling be persistent, not a pest. Come to terms with the reality, that invariably No means No Now not Never, just don't hassle people.

Profit

Profit is not cash and cash is not profit.

Profit is the money that is left, when you take out all the expenses, cost of goods sold and other accounting costs, from how much you sold (less the GST).

Because of the accounting standards and reporting time frames, you may be showing a profit and still have less cash at bank.

You need to understand your numbers, you need to love your numbers and MUST NOT NEGLECT THE NUMBERS.

Use your accountant, to help you with understanding the key aspects of Profit, the difference between Trading/ Gross Profit, Net Profit and EBITDA.

Q is for

Questions

The only bad question is the unasked one. Question everything. If you are unsure, ask why?

If you don't like the answer, or think the respondent is being evasive, repeat. Play broken record, until you have the answer that you know to be true, then say thank you and take the required action.

If you are a sales dude, your role is to ask questions, have the client feel the need to work with you, because you are problem solver first, salesperson second. Just because you have something to sell, doesn't mean that they will buy today. If they have a need and you can fill it, they will buy. It may be now or later. If not now, unless you show up again and ask another question, one thing is certain, someone else will make a sale.

Quick To Act

In a gunfight, the winner usually acts first. and is a good shot.

There are any number of reasons to be quick in business. To be first to market, with an imperfect product, you have the lead, on someone who has a perfect product, but is second or third. As long as the product does not claim to be perfect that is. Then you must continue to do the work on refining the product.

Think about the IT sector; in their world, version 1.0 is an excuse for not having to say you are sorry. Whilst I don't advocate that, if you have an idea that you reckon is worthy, go for it.

Act quickly to get it out there safely and then act, just as quickly, to correct any deficiencies identified and continue to refine it.

R is for

Rapport

Rapport is what is built, with people, when you are prepared to engage, to be vulnerable, to display humility and a willingness to listen and learn.

I have a saying that for you to reveal you to me, I must reveal me to you.

Think about that for a moment. How on earth can you build Rapport, with someone when you don't show up, as who you really are.

Are you prepared to share your thoughts, experiences, successes and failures? If not, it will be harder to build rapport.

Note here. Most people I have met (narcissists aside) relate to people, who can be vulnerable and share their failures. We learn more from mistakes than success.

Responsibility

When you are in business, you have many responsibilities, that you automatically and happily assume and some that you begrudgingly assume. Paying staff the right wages and lodging their superannuation, are automatic, so is paying suppliers on time.

Paying tax is not something you do happily, but necessarily. If there is something that I have learnt the hard way, is that unless you are on

top of tax from day 1, it will be something that can control you and become a sticking point.

Just like a new parent bringing home their first child on the first day, responsibilities are to be embraced and celebrated. They are not a noose hanging around your neck.

Review Your Business- As the Owner

Reviewing your business as the owner, means to look at your business, as to whether it is doing for you, what you want it to.

Question whether you are getting the right type of return, personally, emotionally and financially.

- You may be generating enough money, and still not getting the satisfaction that you need. If so ask why? and then seek to correct that.

- You may be getting great joy and not generating the money. Again ask that question why? Look at the numbers, look at what factors may be impacting the success, what might be keeping customers at bay and what levers you can pull to change the answers.

Approach your business with restless discontent and review constantly.

Review Your Business - As the Customer Sees It

This may sound obvious, but what does your customer see, hear and think that about you, your staff and your business in general that you don't know? And if you did what would you do about it?

Example

I love a cafe as much as most people. I was sitting with my dad recently, at a cafe, in the Outer East of Melbourne. While we were sitting there, I said to Dad, how long do you reckon it is that the owner of this place sat outside as a customer?

The reason for this, is that we were looking at the entry to the cafe. The glass doors were filthy, the frames of the doors, had a large build-up of dirt, grime and general neglect, there was a dustpan and brush and floor mop, hanging off the other glass door, that was visible from the outside, there were cobwebs on the windows and the footpath had not seen a wash, in a very long time.

Now, this cafe was charging top dollar for coffees, breakfast and other food. They were busy, so it may be easy for the owner, to sit back and do nothing about the image, that the cafe portrays, to a new customer.

However, in an environment, as hotly contested as cafes, I would think, that it is not too long, before someone comes along and does it better and affects their successful business.

The things I pointed out to dad, are not earth shattering, and they may not mean anything, but they could also represent a complacency, that is the start of a decline. I guess time will tell.

Example

I was with a friend, in a very busy high street location. He said he wanted to look at a shop, that he has an association with. We stood outside this store. My first impression, was that the shop front, had no relationship to what they sell.

The double fronted shop, with a central door, had plants in the window. This was not a plant shop, it was a liquor store, mostly selling wine. A single light box, on the awning, was the only thing that indicated the brand. The branding, as good as it is, doesn't represent the type of business on the inside. The glass was dirty, there were unrelated and unauthorised stickers, on the tiled facade.

It made me ask my friend "how much business are they missing out on?" It also prompted me to ask, how long since anyone had looked at it, other than the team members working there.

In the months since that conversation, the store has cleaned the glass, removed the unauthorised stickers and placed relevant branding, with see through signage, on the glass.

I don't know whether those actions have improved sales, but I am sure more people know what the store sells now.

You may not be in a wine store, cafe or other food business and think these examples don't apply to you. You would be wrong.

Irrespective of the type of business you have, it is vital that you sit outside your business regularly and look at what your customers see. You might just be surprised and not always pleasantly.

S is for

Sales

Without sales, there is no business, just a dream.

With the advent of social media many things have changed, we can search and compare online (I love the compare the meerkats campaign), we are able to distil some important conversations down to 125 characters, we can make purchases 24/7, from anywhere around the world, while we are in bed, on the train, in our pyjamas and while we are walking. Yep, today consumers have so many choices, they don't know what to do.

If you sell B2B however, there are still some things that have not changed. A good service business can still sell with some of the old principles such as "6 to 9 times of contact with a prospect will equal a customer". Unless of course you just try and do it with social media.

How you construct and manage the contact with a customer, will determine how quickly and how complete a sale will be. If you want a long-term relationship, you will need to establish **rapport, love and trust** and from where I stand, this is only done with true interaction.

Self-Doubt, aka Impostor Syndrome

The most destructive thing, for a business person, is self-doubt. Big Call I know.

Am I worthy?, Am I good enough? Am I full of crap? Am I any good at this? Or the reverse, is my old line to myself, "It's not rocket science, anyone can do this!"

This thinking has caused me more grief, than I can put my hands on.

If you are suffering, from Self Doubt or Impostor Syndrome, do your best to ignore it.

Stop reading about the Cool Kids, who are, or claim to be making millions of dollars, as Influencers, stop doom scrolling on Facebook, Insta, LinkedIn, Tik Tok or any other social space.

Speak authentically, to someone you know you can trust, open up, speak about your fears and doubts, don't ask them to make you feel better, ask them to listen, with empathy. Speaking to someone, doesn't mean that you are seeking advice. Let them know that if you want advice, you will ask for it.

If you haven't got a coach, or a therapist, get one.

Most of all, take the time to nourish yourself, check in on your mental wellbeing, check in on your business and understand that, in order to experience the good times, you have to know the bad.

Lesson

I started business coaching in 2003, branched into Leadership Development in 2009. People I worked with, coached with and beside felt that I was pretty good at both.

Then self-doubt smacked me in the mouth and in 2012, had what I called, my first major episode of impostor syndrome.

Inexplicably, I crashed and burned and panicked about survival, being able to pay the mortgage and other bills that kept the family going. In 12 months, turnover fell by 60%, I would sit for hours in my office, pretending that I was working and effectively paralysed by fear and self-doubt.

I didn't get real with my coach. I felt that they would judge me, because they appeared, to have it all together.

I regressed to a consulting role, where someone else would need to generate the work, that I would carry out. In 2014, I was sick of traveling as much as I was and went back into the cleaning sector. There I was for 5 years, until I had an accident, which changed everything.

In 2019, I left the partnership that I was in. I decided to take a sabbatical of sorts, maybe drive Uber and get a job at Bunnings. Covid 19 changed that course.

Over the next 5 years or so, I languished, unable to explain what I was doing, which was not much really, as I had no confidence, no drive and I was recovering from a significant shoulder injury and mental health issues.

Mental Health, is something some people find uncomfortable to listen to, and others with their own mental health issues, find difficult to speak about and / or allow others to know about. For me, it is just part of me and if you can't accept me for me, that is your problem, not mine.

The accident has eventually had its blessings as I am now sitting here writing, planning on regenerating my work to help others and am working on a few little projects

Moral of this story, get authentic, know that your struggles are very similar to other people's and more importantly, not everyone has their own stuff together all the time, so why should you?

Shareholders' Agreement

This is the legal bit, between you and your partners.

People who are in business together ,without a shareholders' agreement, are setting themselves up, to have a costly and drawn-out argument, about who gets what, in the event of a breakup.

This is the Rules of the Game, the who gets what, how, when, where and why.

There are more stories of bad blood between former partners and family members, when circumstances change, than you can poke a stick at.

Avoid this by having a very Good Shareholders Agreement, that is drawn up, before you even start. Think about this, if you cannot agree before you have entered a relationship, you will have next to no chance of agreeing when, circumstances change and someone wants out.

Shareholding or Profit Share

It is quite likely that, as your business grows and shows some results, that you will want to employ people, some of them will be very good people and be valuable contributors to your success.

It is also likely that you will want to share with them some of that success and that they will hope to share in that success.

The dilemma you might face then is the concept of shares in the business.

Do you give shares away, sell shares to someone or do you agree to a profit share.

As I have learnt, from my own experience as an employee who was promised shares (more of that another time) and also observed as a coach, the matter of issuing shares is no straight forward thing to do, either paid or gifted (earned through sweat equity).

An accountant, is better placed to give advice on this and if you do go down this path, seeing your accountant is a MUST DO, as there are tax implications, as well as legal matters, that need to be considered, planned for and set up.

Sometimes it may be better to reward people with a profit share, that is effectively paid as a bonus to that person, than to issue shares.

Tip

A piece of cautionary advice……. Until you know which way you are going to proceed, DO NOT mention to the person or people you are considering doing this for, that you are planning on doing this.

It sets up an expectation in that person that things will happen. It can lead to false hope and ultimately a disgruntled person if that idea does not materialise.

The road of good intention is paved with many disappointed skeletons, both the well-intended owner and the aggrieved employee.

<u>**YOU MUST HAVE YOUR ACCOUNTANT TO ADVISE YOU ON THIS.**</u>

Structure

This is one of the most important decisions you will make, and it is not about whether you build your home, in brick or timber.

The type of Company/ Business Structure, you and your accountant (yes I said accountant) decide to operate in, will determine a lot about how, you move forward.

Some options are a Sole Trader, A Family Trust, a Proprietary Limited Company, a Partnership.

Things like Tax Registration, how you pay yourself and others, if that is what you are planning.

<u>**YOU MUST SEEK ADVICE FROM ACCOUNTANTS AND LAWYERS**</u>

Superannuation / Financing Your Retirement

In Australia, Paul Keating (former Treasurer and Prime Minister) initiated the Superannuation Guarantee Levy as a way to have all Australians provide for their own retirement. The aim being, to eventually remove the Commonwealth Pension and Social Security Scheme.

A great idea. And for employees of companies, it works beautifully and eventually there will be a low dependency of Commonwealth resources to keep people alive.

But what happens to you, as a business owner or self-employed person or maybe a gig worker, often scratching out a living, or using your money on things, that you see are essential to future proofing the business?

The Sale of the Business will be your super! Right?

Possibly but maybe not. Many businesses are unsalable, so the expectation of being able to cash out and wack that cash into super to fund retirement, does not eventuate.

Unless you have been disciplined and transferred money to your super account every month, you may turn around, after 20 years and find, that your super balance is very low and unlikely to support your retirement.

Whatever you do, just as you will do for Tax, you MUST put aside super funds, to get the benefit of compounding interest over the next 5,10, 20 years.

Speak to your accountant, about how much you should put away.

ALPHABITE SOUP FOR BUSINESS

T is for

Taxation

There are only two things certain in life, death and taxes.

How pervasive tax issues are for you, will be up to you and your accountant (ultimately you are the one who signs the declaration to the Tax Office, be sure about what you are signing).

A good rule of thumb, is that 40-50% of every dollar you make, after expenses will go to the taxman, no way to avoid that.

There is an obligation to yourself, to ensure that you pay, only what you must pay. Legitimate minimisation, NOT avoidance.

> **Example**
>
> There was a famous interaction, between Kerry Packer (now deceased) and a Government Committee, who were accusing him of not paying enough tax. He was very, very, wealthy and very, very, very powerful and from reports over the years, very scary to deal with.
>
> In the hearing he said to the Committee, that it was his (and yours by extension) duty, to pay as little tax as possible, so that they had less of his (yours) money to waste.
>
> He was armed, with great Lawyers and Accountants and was able to legally minimise his tax, as opposed to avoiding, which would be illegal.

In Australia, we have this thing that you may have heard about, GST. It is the Goods and Services Tax and is paid by everyone on almost all sales.

Depending on your structure, you may need to lodge a GST return at least quarterly, or maybe monthly.

Whatever you do and as much as it will annoy you, lodge and pay on time. The Tax Office, is a very forceful body and will be your nemesis, if you don't play by their rules.

Whichever way you slice it, pay your tax. Be like Packer and get a good accountant, to help you pay, only what you're obliged to.

Tax Provisioning

Continuing on from above, I have said that 40-50% of everything you make, is the Tax Office's.

When the end of the year comes along and it's time to square up with the Tax Office, and you have a big bill to pay and you have not provisioned for that tax, the stress you will be under, will be enormous.

So, what do you do about avoiding that stress?

Have a dedicated Tax Bank Account for a starter. Try and get one that will gather interest.

Once you have established that account, from every payment you receive, (if a service business) transfer 30% of that payment. No exceptions, no matter what else you have going on. Be Disciplined.

I know that may sound over the top, but speaking from experience and from other friends, who have done similar to me, when you spend everything in the main bank account, even if it is just to keep your head above water, when the taxman comes knocking, blind panic and massive regret will visit you.

In my case, it was the trigger for me to go into a massive depressive episode, that took months to come out of, in which time my sales crashed.

Time
The Time to think.

Quiet contemplation is often overlooked as a necessary part of our lives, as we go harder than ever before, to get more done, in less time.

Meditation, Relaxation, Yoga, Pilates, Exercise, whatever is your thing, is your thing. Whatever works best for you, is best for you. There is no right or wrong.

But what about when you are in a meeting, not present, immersed in "stuff" and you are asked to answer a question, you may be caught off guard? My suggestion is to allow yourself a pause, a nano second, some time to think. You may even want to say, "Great question, I am unsure, can I get back to you on that?", You may just need a second or two to allow the question to fully embed.

By taking a second or so, the person asking the question is likely to think that you are thoughtful, considerate and have listened to them. That is a good thing.

The Time to act

Give yourself time to act. Overcommitment is a killer and sets you up for stressful delivery. If you think something will take you 2 hours, ask for 3 or more. As humans, we have a tendency to overestimate how much we can get done and therefore over promise and often under deliver.

Rarely are we expected to make time driven, life and death decisions in our work, unless you are in a 1st responders' role, so why put yourself under undue pressure, which could lead to mistakes.

The Time to work hard

There is a time for working hard and a time for working smart.

When you are young and in early stages of your career, or your business, it is very hard to differentiate the two and often harder, not smarter, is what transpires, as you try to get more done, get more Kudos, or get that next promotion or deal.

As a person, who has historically been "Guilty Your Honour", I can assure you, that the means do not justify the end. Yes, that is what I meant to say.

I was an 80 hour a week dude, for a very long time, giving everything to my work, my bosses, my community, to anyone who I thought mattered, except for my family, friends and myself.

Fortunately for me, my family is intact, my gorgeous wife of nearly 40 years, my two adult children and granddaughter still love me. My mental health suffered, my fitness suffered and relationships with friends were strained, at times, because I was so busy, being busy.

The Time to relax,
I like to say that there are No Pockets on a Shroud.

There are plenty of people in the Cemetery who died rich and exhausted, while they chased their next dollar/ next win/ next big deal.

Spending time to relax and just BE, are essential to our lives.

Plan time for you, your family, your friends, a walk in the forest, or on the beach.

The Time to play
As with relaxing, being able to play, when the time is right, is key to a balanced life.

I love the footy (Australian Rules Football) I love watching my team, Essendon, play when they are winning (not so much when not winning).

What is best about that, is the times I watch them, with my family or my mates. Over time, I have worked out, that it is not the footy, that gets me excited, but being with family and friends.

Make time for Play.

TLAs - Three Letter Acronyms (or more)

Jargon and internal language are often used to shorten conversations and sometimes to confuse outsiders. Governments, Corporates and Institutions, are really good at them.

Knowing what they are and when to use them, is helpful if not essential. It might have saved my Boss, from killing our chance to win that Mining Cleaning Contract (See Humility and LTIs)

You will know doubt see hundreds, including KPI, KRA, P&L, EBITDA, PTI. If you want more, check out the Glossary of TLAs

It is worth cautioning you against using them, with everyone you encounter, so as not to confuse them, or make them feel less worthy of you.

Tough Calls

With ownership comes responsibility. Easily said hey? Not so easy to do however, for many of us.

Rest assured, making Tough Calls, is one of the most important things, you will need to do, as you navigate being in business.

Your family, your future self and business survival depend on it.

When faced with a tough call on an employee, procurement of any type, a supplier relationship, or a client who you just don't feel is right for you, face up to this FACT.

Your money is at stake and your family needs you, to make tough calls.

Trust

Trust is something we all need, whether it be Trust in a product, a service, a person, the Government.

The thing that you need to be sure of is that YOU CAN BE TRUSTED, that you can be relied upon, to come through with the goods, when needed, that your product, will do what you say it will do and most importantly for you to turn up on time.

Trusted Advisors

There are few people who can do everything, or be good at everything.

When you are in business, it can be very lonely, isolating and having you feel like an Island.

It doesn't need to be that way.

Building a team of advisors around you, to support you, challenge you, your thoughts and beliefs is as an important part of being in business, as getting up in the morning and eating breakfast.

Sure, they should care about you as a person and in doing that, must not tolerate your BS. They must have your permission, to be brutally frank with you, to have you put up your argument as to why you are doing something.

Mine over the years have included, my accountants, financial planner, lawyer, successful business people I have met from my volunteering, a successful AFL Coach, friends in business, mentors.

Build your Trusted Advisory Team and listen intently
.

U is for

Universal Truths

Sometimes called universal principles, that is, that they are True in almost all cases. Some examples below

6-9 times contact = a client

There is no such thing as, Good Fast and Cheap

The universal principle of lag, where the time from starting an activity, to it having an impact, is generally 90 days

ROSS S MITCHELL

V is for

Values

You could take this a number of ways, what value, is the service I am offering? am I being of value to the person, the team, whatever?

Or you could take it, as being, what are my values? Things like Integrity, Fairness, Reliability, Responsibility, Dependability.

The list of things, that could be YOUR values, is huge and should be unique to you.

Your values should be, what YOU STAND FOR, What YOU ARE KNOWN FOR and they should be the same, in your business, as they are in your life.

Once you have established what they are, find people who meet YOUR values, customers, clients and staff, friends and supporters.

Vision

Ghandi said that "without hope the people will perish". I reckon that without Vision the business will perish.

One of the most important tools, that I have used as a coach, is to have people complete a Vision exercise. It considers all the realms of the business owner's life, not just their business.

The realms include Family, Finances, Wealth, Exercise, Spirit, Business, Legacy. You may want to add more in.

The Vision exercise is described in The Big Why

Victim

Don't be a victim of falling for a sucker scheme, from a Nigerian bank, telling you that your long lost uncle in Yorkshire, left you £400 million and then give them your bank account details.

Use the best internet security you can and protect your details.

Don't get sucked in to paying for things, that you might be able to do yourself, if it provides an ROYT (return on your time)

Don't get sucked in to thinking, that you can do things, in half the time, that someone is wanting to charge you fair market rate for. Pay the professional

Don't do the $25 an hour work yourself when you can charge out 2, 3 or even 10 times that yourself and then complain that you have no time to make sales. Hire a PA

Volunteering

This is something that we all have an ability to do. That might mean, helping cook snags, at the Bunnings Sausage Sizzle, for your soccer club once a year. Or it might take, a much more serious form, where you put your talents to best use.

It can also be a place, where you get to build an amazing pool of great people around you.

Some of my best connections, in Business and Life, have come from being a volunteer. I have grown a network of people who I can trust, rely on in times of need, ask for a referral to someone I want to meet, or to a service that I need to procure.

W is for

Wasted Energy
One of the greatest energy sappers in business, is the person who brings nothing to the table,

They are the energy vampire. They suck you dry and leave you feeling like you would rather eat you own arm off, than meet with them.

Tip.
Set them free. Cut them from your life,
You don't need them.

If they're a client, ask yourself, what are they bringing to you? If they bring less than they take, maybe, they would be better working with someone else. If they are staff, let them work somewhere else.

Life is too short, for unnecessary misery, so when you find yourself working with an energy vampire, get out.

If you are in business with that person and you are fearful of losing what you have invested, whether it be time, money, energy or your reputation, the advice is the same, get out. That time, money, effort and reputation are already compromised, gone, or in the process of going.

Once you do say "sayonara", you will quickly learn, that no amount of you expecting them to change, would have made a single bit of difference.

People like this have no moral compass, no self-awareness (yet they think they do, can also be known as narcissists) and will keep on sucking until there is no more and then make you the worst person in the world for abandoning them.

ROSS S MITCHELL

X is for

X factor

When you have something better than the ordinary to give you could have the x factor.

I don't believe that it is specifically measurable, but you know it when you see it.

ROSS S MITCHELL

Y is for

Y is Without a doubt the best question you can ask

Yes

Yes I can do it,
Yes you can have it
Of course I can
Yes it will be done today

Just as I have said you must learn to say NO, you must equally apply the response YES to your repertoire.

Yes is a pathway to testing yourself, and don't forget that while you are saying YES, remember the Good Fast and Cheap principle must be applied.

"Yes you can have it tomorrow. Ordinarily your request would take 3 days, so, so it will cost a little more. Are you OK with that?

You Matter

If not for you then who?

The following example should help you understand why YOU Matter

> I was in a café in Shanghai in 2007 and looked out the window and saw two famous Australians, standing in the street.
>
> Sadly, both have since passed away.
>
> Max Walker was a big proud Victorian, who played VFL Football for Melbourne and more famously playing Cricket, as fast bowler for Victoria and Australia.
>
> I had met Max a few weeks earlier, at an event for a

client of mine. Max was the keynote speaker and we shook hands and spoke only briefly on the night.

Max was in Shanghai, with another equally famous former VFL/ AFL player and coach and Hall Of Fame member, Ron Barassi.

I could not help myself and thought this is too good to be true, Max and Ron in Shanghai, what are the odds? (about 19million to one really) so I went outside and said G'day.

Before I could say anything more, Max says to me, "it's Ross isn't it? We met a few weeks ago at that event." I was surprised by him remembering me. It was what he said next that is had me write this.

He said "you are the business coach working with XYZ Company, and they say that you are doing a great job". I was blown away that he had remembered that and would even feel the need to say that.

Then, he introduced me to Ron, who could sense my surprise that Max remembered me.

Ron was larger than life and famous for his sayings. He just said "it is great to meet you and remember these 20 letters, **"IF IT IS TO BE IT IS UP TO ME"**.

We shook hands and wished each other a good week in China.

It is important that you understand that You matter to more people than you will ever know or understand.

No matter who you are, no matter how famous, or not, you are, you do not know how much impact you can have on others, by being you, by being authentic and operating without expectation.

Z is for

Zany

Not all weird ideas are bad, some of the most ridiculous ideas, can produce a result.

The world of Professional golf, was thrown into disarray, a few years ago with the LIV golf tour.

Traditional PGA golf tournaments are played over 4 rounds over 4 days. They are traditional, quiet and somewhat predictable in format. Spectators are required to remain quiet, so players can concentrate. Players must wear long pants, there is a cut, after 2 rounds, so only half the field plays on the weekend, when more spectators could get value for money. Players only get paid if they make the cut.

LIV golf allows players to wear shorts, they play as a team as well as an individual, they are paid, win, lose or draw, based on their contract, and when they win, they get bonuses. The tournaments are played Friday, Saturday and Sunday with all players playing. Spectators have the chance to be rowdy, they have party holes and everything seems a lot more fun.

"If we do what we have always done we get what we have always gotten"

Throw your open arms around a Zany idea and see what happens. Just remember, to fail early and fail often

Zealous

When you know who your ideal customers are you will stop hunting for everyone who is not

The number of people I have encountered over the years who are in sales, and I asked them who their ideal client is, they start with anybody who!

To that, I say, anybody, everybody, somebody, but really that means nobody. Hit and Hope or Spray and Prey is not a strategy to win.

"When all you have is a hammer everything looks like a nail"

It is crucial that as a business owner, you be zealous about who you want to work with.

If you are looking for a new job, it is not any job, it is a specific job. If you are seeking a new car, it is a specific car, not just any car

If you are looking for a new client, you need to be able to say:
- what that client looks like,
- what their interest is in your service or product,
- why they should buy from you,
- how much you would like to sell to them,
- what their personality type is.

Let's just say, that you sell genuine high-end watches, Rolex, Omega, Patek Phillipe. You know that your watches are selling for more than

$10,000. Do you try and sell that brand of watch from the boot of the car, or in Facebook marketplace, to every person who happens to be online, or on the Home shopping network?.

Probably not.

Your likely customer, has a high level of disposable income, possibly travels for work, or shops in the High Street of a capital city, or has someone in their life, that does that for them. You put your store in

Collins Street Melbourne, Pitt Street Mall Sydney, International Airports and advertise on Digital signage in Airport Lounges, Airline Magazines, the Major Finance Magazines and the like. Same with a Luxury car brand.

It really does not matter what it is you sell, you need to understand specifically who is not your ideal client as much as who is your ideal client. That way, you can invest time effort and energy into making, the highest possible sales, from the least possible effort, with service that delights..

Pursue that with the Zeal of a Lion chasing its optimum prey, the Zebra and you should start to see the results you are chasing.

ROSS S MITCHELL

�
Where to Next? The Final Word

Now that you have got to the end, what is next?

Hopefully this book, as small as it is, as simplistic as it is (and I suspect that some people will possibly regard it as being too simplistic),

I recommend that you consider the following steps, to take into the next phase of your business. If it is your career most of the list below applies in some form.

- make a date with yourself, to assess whether you really want this.
- be clear and honest with yourself, about whether you are prepared to do what it takes to succeed.
- write out, draw or type up your personal goals
- establish whether you have the immediate skills, to do what it is you hope to make a success of
    - if yes, go build a business plan
    - if no, go get the help you need, a coach, a mentor, the correct education/ skills development. I am not saying enrol for an MBA here and wait another 4 years. Work out the gaps you have and fill the biggest, most relevant one, then develop a business plan. Tip for you. You will not need to be a finance guru yourself, and you will still need to have one. The skills, I am referring to, are related to whatever it is, you are going to sell, make or do.
- do the necessary research, to show that there is a market.
- engage professional advisors, accountant, legal, marketing/ branding experts. **Whatever you pay now, will be way less than what you pay later to correct mistakes that are long embedded.**

- register your business.
- open at least one bank account, in your business name. I recommend 2 accounts, 1 for trading and 1 for tax provisioning.
- get a domain name.
- get social. Online and Physical
- build a brand, get a logo developed by a professional.
- build your personal and professional profile.
- decide how you will invoice, charge and collect payment for your work.
- get a cloud-based, financial software account. I love Xero. It is easy to use and intuitive for non-accountants.
- launch your business.
- be patient and persistent.
- join a networking group, or 2 or 3 or 4.
- as you go along, keep filling the gaps, that you identified at the start, as well as the ones that you start to notice that you didn't identify earlier.

Most importantly you MUST KNOW THIS!

Business can be hugely satisfying and gratifying, it can be equally and sometimes more frustrating and disappointing. It is definitely a roller coaster.

Just as a roller coaster gets you to experience, exhilaration, so will your business, but you MUST be prepared for the tough times, that will inevitably come. How you handle those, will determine whether you keep going, when everything in you says stop.

Being a business owner can be lonely. Sometimes your family won't get you, or understand why you are doing it. They may even start to encourage you to give up. If that is what you are looking for, then that will be OK, but if you are fully committed, that is the time that you need people around you to support you. Get a tribe, your tribe.

Do what Ian Thorpe did, engage a Coach or a mentor, who is going to keep you on point.

MOST IMPORTANTLY. ENJOY THE RIDE

Best wishes to your great success

-Ross

<u>NOT THE END</u>
<u>THIS SHOULD ONLY BE THE BEGINNING!</u>

ROSS S MITCHELL

About The Author

Ross Mitchell lives in Melbourne, Australia, is married to Shuana, his wife and partner in life for nearly 40 years, They have 2 adult children, Ashlee and Sam, who are both married. and a gorgeous granddaughter Daisy.

Ross has worked in a wide array of roles throughout his career.

From Selling Papers at 11 years of age, to being a part owner of a cleaning business and being respected, as a leading business coach for 13 years, Ross' journey to 60 has not all been smooth sailing.

Ross is a Subject Matter Expert on Facility Services Contracts and a Specialist Generalist Business Coach and Consultant, with the ability to coach business and people across multiple industries and roles.

Ross has said that his "MBA doesn't hang proudly on his wall, because he doesn't have one and the only time he has been to university is to look at Cleaning Contracts". For a long time that was the reality It is only partially true now, as he has consulted to a large number of Universities on their facility services contracts and has even been a sessional lecturer at Box Hill Institute.

Ross has openly discussed the struggles that he has had with mental health, PTSD and the personal injury, that had him walk away from the spotlight of business ownership in 2019.

In the time since then, he has had a sort of sabbatical from business life.

He spent 2 years at Bunnings, ran a small Handyman business, had a crack at Acting (a couple of small parts in TV commercials and Extras roles in Mini Series') and after 2 years of working hard on his mental Health, has returned to share his vast, no nonsense business experience in a book called Alphabite Soup for Business.

Alphabite Soup is a pragmatic, read as much, or as little as you like, guide to business, some of it for the never ending number of people, who have an idea and are looking at starting a business, but have no idea where to start, or for those more experienced business people, who are simply for a quick reference, or some reassurance that what they are doing is right.

Ross' hope is that whatever you are doing, in coming to this book, or his work, that you are able to apply what you learn, to make a better life for you and your family

Follow Ross on
LinkedIn. rossmitchell1264
YouTube. rossmitchell4469
Instagram. rossmitchell64
Facebook. australiasbestbusinesscoach Reach out via email to ross@nesso.com.au

Acknowledgements

Over my 40 odd years of working, there are plenty of people I could thank, for their contribution to me at a professional and personal level.

It is the work in Leadership and Coaching that has had the most profound impact, on my ability to be able to write this book.

During my period as a full time coach, I was associated with a number of groups who, I either trained with, worked with, became accredited or licenced in their processes. There is no doubt that I was able to learn an amazing array of tools from them.

Thanks to the team at Mindshop, led by Chris and Julie Mason and their family, including Emily and James. Inside the Mindshop family further thanks to some great people I had there to support me, especially Mike Burke, Russell Cummings and Mike Boyle.

Thanks also go to the team at Integrity and Values led by Jennifer and Jay Elliott.

Thanks also to Jeff Muir for tough love.

I have mentioned Cliff Dawson from the Whitehorse Business Group Saward Dawson (now retired) for your mentoring, friendship and continued counsel.

There are many more I could thank. I sincerely hope that you know who you are and what your input has meant to me.

ROSS S MITCHELL

ALPHABITE SOUP FOR BUSINESS

Three Letter Acronyms-
bonus list

Just because you work somewhere, doesn't always mean you know what things mean, just ask a Doctor, a Government worker or a military person.

The world is full of Jargon, some useful, some transferable to most people and almost always it has a possibility to create confusion to the uninitiated.

Below you will find a list of TLAs, not an exhaustive list by any means and it is still quite large.

If you can grasp most of them, you will have an advantage over those who don't.

Please don't be too cute with them and deliberately try to bamboozle people, so that you can show them just how clever you are.

But do have a little fun.

TLA	**Stands For**	**What I Reckon It Means**
AAP	Australian Associated Press	Good to know if you want to get newsworthy info out. Not good if you muck up, as they may go after you
ABN	Australian Business Number	Unique identifier to the ATO for every person who is a sole trader, registered businesses- can include companies. Used everywhere. Banks Government, Credit providers etc.

TLA	Stands For	What I Reckon It Means
ACCC	Australian Competition and Consumer Commission	The people who are supposed to monitor business on behalf of consumers. Especially around pricing practices.
ACN	Australian Company Number	Same as ABN, but only for companies and trusts
AI	Artificial Intelligence	It used to only be as smart as the programmer…... Maybe not now. Friend or Foe?, a little bit from column a and a little bit from column b
ASIC	Australian Securities and Investments Commission	The people who are supposed to monitor business practices and ownership
ATO	Australian Taxation Office	The main Government Collection Agency in Australia, www.ato.gov.au
BAS	Business Activity Statement	The work you do in collecting tax on your sales for the ATO and your monthly or quarterly report- see GST
BoD	Board of Directors	They tell the Big Boss what they want the business to do.
BPM	Business Process Mapping	Recording how you do stuff, so that you can create SOP
CAC	Customer Acquisition Cost	How much you spend to acquire a customer. How much you spend will depend on knowing the LTV
CDEO	Chief Diversity and Equity	The Diversity and Equity Boss

ALPHABITE SOUP FOR BUSINESS

TLA	Stands For	What I Reckon It Means
	Officer	
CDO	Chief Digital Officer	The CMOs Digital elf (needs the title to feel important)
CEO	Chief Executive Officer	The Big Boss
CEW	Chief Executive Women	The Boss to champion Women
CFA	Cash Flow Analysis	Gives you a picture of when, or if, you are heading towards a cliff. Ignore this and you might need to put on a parachute to slow the fall
CFO	Chief Finance Officer	The Finance Boss
CHO	Chief Health Officer	The one person you did not want to do a press conference during Co-Vid Crisis
CIO	Chief Information Officer	The IT Boss
CLO	Chief Legal Officer	The Lawyer Boss- sometimes known as Internal Counsel
CMO	Chief Marketing Officer	The Marketing Boss
CMO	Chief Medical Officer	The Boss of Medical stuff- more likely to be a government dude
CoB	Chairman of the Board	The Bigger Boss of the BoD or EB. Used to be Frank Sinatra's monicker.
COGS	Cost of Goods Sold	What you spent on things you sell
COO	Chief Operating Officer	The Operations Boss

TLA	Stands For	What I Reckon It Means
CQO	Chief Quality Officer	The Boss of Quality Control
CRM	Customer Relationship Management	Usually relates to a system used for tracking and growing sales and customer activity
		Also a critical thing to keep doing
CRO	Chief Revenue Officer	The Sales Boss
CSO	Chief Sustainability Officer	The Green Boss.
CTR	Click Through Rate	Tracking customer behaviour on your digital platforms, to work out what they like and what they don't
DM	Direct Message/ing	This means not needing to speak to someone. Just DM Me!
DM	Direct Marketing/ Direct Mail	How everyone used to do business, still works for some- look at your fridge for a plumber, electrician, handyman, pizza shop, Chinese restaurant or your real estate agents' footy fixture
DoGE	Department of Government Efficiency	Donald Trump and Elon Musk's version of let's fix government overspending. Time will tell if this is a good or bad thing
EA	Executive Assistant (TLA of 2 letters)	The Bosses' helpers- think of them as Santa's elves
EB	Executive Board	They tell the Big Boss what they have to do

ALPHABITE SOUP FOR BUSINESS

TLA	**Stands For**	**What I Reckon It Means**
ELG	Executive Leadership Group	When most of the Chiefs get together and form strategy that the EB or BoD, told the Big Boss to do
EMDG	Export Market Development Grant	If you make stuff and want to sell Overseas, these guys might help with some cash. See www.austrade.gov.au
EPS	Earnings Per Share	You want lots if a Shareholder
EQ	Emotional Intelligence	Internal emotional smarts- HI EQ=empathy(you know your impact on others), Low EQ= narcissistic tendencies (you have no idea on and don't care about your impact on others)
ESL	English as a Second Language	With the expansion of multiculturalism, needing to cater for people with ESL, is critical to business success. Basically, your business process needs to (or must) cater for people, whose 1st language is not yours
FAQ	Frequently Asked Questions	There will be many
FTA	Free Trade Agreement	Rules agreed to trade between countries. Most People and Governments respect them, some don't- just check on USA 2025 and Trump Tariff changes
FWC	Fair Work Commission	The Employment Umpire in Australia

TLA	Stands For	What I Reckon It Means
GST	Goods and Services Tax	The government's claws out on everything you sell
IAS	Income Activity Statement	Your report for the ATO, on the work you do in collecting tax on your declared income. A truly thankless task.
IDK	I Don't Know	A sign of humility- followed up with IWFO. I will find out.
IQ	Intelligence Quotient	Not really that important unless you are in a contest to show how smart you are. Highly regarded by Intellects and Narcissists
IT	Information Technology	You are using it. Where would we be without it?
IWD	International Women's Day	A day in March, to Acknowledge how important women's contribution to everything is.
IWFO	I Will Find Out	Follow up to IDK. Essential.
KPI	Key Performance Indicator	Lots of these
KRA	Key Result Area	Less Of These
LAN	Local Area Network	Moving digital stuff internally- works without the internet
LTV	Life-Time Value	How much a customer gives you (sales or profit) over the time they deal with you

ALPHABITE SOUP FOR BUSINESS

TLA	Stands For	What I Reckon It Means
MC	Master of Ceremonies	A good one will make your event run seamlessly; a not so good one will make your event memorable for the wrong reasons
MD	Managing Director	The Big Boss of a Private Company
MoU	Memorandum of Understanding	Record of what has been agreed to- legally important
NBN	National Broadband Network	Australia's internet framework- not as good as it could be
NFA	No Further Action	No further comment!
NFP	Not for Profit	Does not mean FOR LOSS, often exempt from tax and usually a charity- incidentally the AFL is an NFP. Go figure
NLP	Neuro Linguistic Programming	Some would say it is witchcraft, good for understanding psychology of sales
NMP	Not My Problem	I just made this one up. But surely used by all politicians and narcissists
OH&S	Occupational Health and Safety	The way we work to keep people safe so that they can go home intact
OTD	On Time Delivery	What you hope to deliver and prey for when you are receiving from a courier
OTD	On Time Departure	Airlines, Trains, Trams and Buses hope for and often miss. You always hope for

TLA	Stands For	What I Reckon It Means
PAYG	Pay As You Go	The Income Tax you pay as you earn.
PNC	People and Culture	The department that looks after employing people and the employees. - Used to be called HR
PPL	Paid Parental Leave	The right of new parents to paid time off
Q&A	Questions and Answers	If you don't ask questions you won't get answers!
ROE	Return on Effort	How much improvement you get for how much effort you put in
ROE	Return on Equity	Similar to ROI
ROI	Return on Investment	How much money you get back for how much you put in
RTW	Right to Work	A fundamental right of everyone, sometimes though we need to remove it for safety
SaaS	Software as a Service	Think cloud-based software- for those not old enough to remember, software used to come in a retail box on floppy disks and had a special key. No renewal no software.
SBO	Small Business Ombudsman	The small business umpire you may need some day
SGL	Superannuation Guarantee Levy	Helping Aussies pay for their retirement. Paid by the employer

ALPHABITE SOUP FOR BUSINESS

TLA	**Stands For**	**What I Reckon It Means**
SOP	Standard Operating Procedures	The way we are supposed to do things
SOP	Someone Else's Problem	I just made this one up. But surely used by all politicians and narcissists
SOW	Scope of Works	Sometimes known as a specification of services
SRO	State Revenue Office	The Local Tax Office
STP	Single Touch Payroll	The transfer of cash from you to employees, Super Funds and ATO
SWMS	Safe Work Method Statements	Your SOP with the safety stuff included
TFN	Tax File Number	Unique identifier to the ATO for every person. Used everywhere. Banks Government, Credit providers etc
UNO	Unplanned Network Outage	Something no-one wants
VIP	Very Important Person	You and everyone you deal with
VPN	Virtual Private Network	Moving digital stuff securely- works internally and externally
WAN	Wider Area Network	Moving digital stuff internally and externally with internet or VPN
WFH	Working From Home	Working in your pyjamas whilst at home- no need to catch the train or drive an hour each way

TLA	Stands For	What I Reckon It Means
WFHH	Working From Home Hybrid	Working in your pyjamas whilst at home 2 or 3 days per week- no need to catch the train or drive an hour each way, on those days. Then working at the office, the other days. Sorry but you need to get dressed for work and catch the train or drive.
WHS	Workplace Health and Safety	The way we work to keep people safe so that they can go home intact
WIP	Work In Progress	Your to do list and critical to monitor when you are running a project
WWCC	Working With Children Check	You may need to have one if you interact with Children. Definitely needed for working in Childcare, Schools, Universities, kids' sports

ALPHABITE SOUP FOR BUSINESS

www.ingramcontent.com/pod-product-compliance
Lightning Source LLC
Chambersburg PA
CBHW040638100526
44583CB00038B/3069